Bleed Them Dry

Sara Rian

...

Published by ...

ISBN 978-1-7247-3323-8

Typesetting services by BOOKOW.COM

to my mother,
thank you for teaching me how to breathe
and how to love.

Epigraph

a blank face in a dream once

asked me about how i love.

i replied with 4 words.

-i bleed them dry

Contents

Blood Play 1
Blood Loss 81

Blood Play

break me.

i love the sound of my bones and heart
shattering.

-masochist

let's drink wine
as dark as our blood
and talk about death
for hours.

-date night

i rummage through boxes and crates full of men
looking for one to torment me like you do.

searching for someone to put their hands on me
and it feel like silk and sandpaper.

you were like needles in my bloodstream
and i won't stop searching for that misery.

-lust and found

you are an entity possessing my body and mind
and i am desperate to cast you out.

i am swallowing handfuls of crystals and stones
in hopes of vibrational calibration.
burning bundles of sacred herbs and sticks.
an attempt to cleanse you from my home and heart.
mumbling questions in front of a deck of cards.
dangling pendulums over symbols and spreads
trying to summon answers.

i am afraid no ritual or spell will exorcise you from me
because there is no force stronger than this

-witchcraft

i do not really love you
because love is not real.
it is a lethal combination of chemicals, a physiological scheme.
you are only a trigger provoking a deadly process.

you arouse dopamine in me and i feel like i am taking hits of you.
it tricks me into thinking you are some euphoric reward.

you cripple my serotonin and i lose the ability to regulate.
i obsess and ruminate over you but you are not worth one thought.

you boost oxytocin and my fatal attachment to you forms.
the final blow and my body's ultimate betrayal.

my brain drenches itself in falsities and illusions.
and i want to carve out the pieces saturated in my own venom.
love is the deadliest cocktail
and i am not sober.

-love poison no. 9

i could lie
and blame these bleeding knees on prayer.
but one sin is enough tonight.

-he is church

take my hand and walk with me into the water.
feel sensation on your skin one last time.
kiss me slowly and steal the last breath from my chest
for our next inhale will respire freedom.

darling, we know we are much too potent for this world
and this is the only way we can be diluted.
let the water engulf us and fill our lungs until they burst.
until our rib cages crack open and only love flows out.

we will rest together on the ocean floor and play with sand.
our bodies teeming with saltwater and tranquility.
just waiting for the moment when our hearts
stop beating   at the   same   time.

-watered down

cut away
these eyelids
and
those clothes.

i want to soak you in

-entirely

marry me in a cemetery
with only death as our witness.
lay me down on tear-soaked grass
and let's rest our heads on tombstones.
we will stay warm with blankets of soil,
and fall asleep reading names no longer spoken.

life on death.
me on you.

-dream wedding

as my body almost surrendered
to his deadly bite
you put your mouth on me
and sucked the venom from my wound.

-extraction

trying to claw myself out of this grave.
fingernails soiled and bleeding
breathe in dirt, exhale hope.
i think my lungs are crushed
and my brain is screaming.
it begs for the suffocation to come
but my body pathetically struggles
to survive this.
i cannot tell if i am digging myself out
or deeper.

and this is what it feels like to love you.

-buried alive

i know this is not said often.
but if we grow old together
i hope you die first.

you have stopped my heart so many times
and i have always wanted to know
what love looks like from the other side.

-my turn

this is only a waiting game.
a countdown to an inevitable ruining.

this could be the calm before the storm.
just before my hurricane self comes on too strong
and rips through your avoidant architecture.
leaving a path of decayed debris and skeletal fragments.

or this is the dangerous dry season.
moments before you spark and combust without warning
and burn me alive like wildfire.
setting me ablaze to be left as smoldering ash and bone.

two beautiful forces waiting to be provoked
and ready to consume.
so darling, let's enjoy the calm, let's enjoy the drought.
for in the end, only one of us will make it out alive.

-natural disasters

i love to melt when i come near your heat.
and you love to mold me into the girl you want.

-made of wax

my fantasy starts with you and me in the sand.
bare and exposed in a deserted paradise.
the sun kissing our skin
and you kissing mine.

the only thing to be heard is the sound of waves
and breaths crashing.
not knowing if the salt we taste
is from the sea or our pores.

you line colorful seashells
from my sternum down my stomach.
as though you are mapping
where you will go next.

your lips reach and touch each one like stepping stones
as you find your way to the spot marked with an "x".

-treasure island

i am quite feral.
i eat food with my hands
and lick the sweat that drips down your neck.
because everything tastes better when you truly indulge.

-carnal pleasure

i am scanning my blood and limbs.
dissecting every layer and membrane.
hoping to locate the places you have festered and corrupted.

i need to carve you out like cancer.
but you have swept through me
and spread to every organ and cell in my body.

i am saturated and declining
but destroying you would be
suicide.

-infection

run your tongue over my wrists and neck
while i pretend it's a razor blade.
i like to split open in more ways than one.

-play pretend

your head on my chest.
not knowing how many times
you've bruised the heart
underneath these ribs.
resting there so oblivious.
all i can feel is
-envy

you fall for the perishable parts of me.
a surface level appeal.
you comment on my appearance and praise these fleeting traits.

but darling
my body will change. my skin will crease.
my hair and energy will grey.

for to really love me is to know me.
to recognize the ceaseless pieces of me that will never dissolve.

if you love me for these things
we will last long after this vessel decays.

-some parts are undying

thank you.
for being the first since the wreck.
to breathe into this lifeless body

making blood pulse through my veins again.
softening and melting this petrified heart.
you revived my ability to love.

i was not your forever, only a moment.
and to you, our endeavor may seem slight.
but to me it was vital.

-resurrected

we cannot always have this
or we wouldn't get so high.
if only for a little while
i knew that you were mine.

now that you are gone
the world appears dull.
but i would rather have a moment
than nothing at all.

-my only rhyme

the most tragic thing to witness
is love breaking
by force of circumstance.

-strong love still breaks

in a parallel universe
you and i woke up together today.

you kissed me and whispered "happy anniversary".
we stayed there for a while holding one another.
sitting in the sunlight beaming through the windows.
moving slower as if it would give us more time.

we hadn't fought months earlier.
you didn't resent me, i hadn't gone numb.
we saw more days, months, anniversaries ahead.

but this is not that universe. it is this one.
this path of dismantling. unraveling. pain.
no more days, months, anniversaries. not together.

you and i suffer on this path as our alternate versions smile.
but it will all be worth it.
this universe will one day be
a slow morning full of love.

not now.
but eventually.

-slow mourning

if you are here looking for sweet words
or waiting for me to compare love to fruit
you've come to the wrong place.

my words are bitter.
love burns and drenches my throat
like vinegar.

-unsweetened

someone once told me
they hoped i would always find darkness in life.
but this was not to wish me ill.

they know anguish is the black mulch i need to survive.
they see how i blossom in melancholy
and flourish in sorrow.

it was the most beautiful response to when i confessed
that my biggest fear is that one day
i would be too happy to write.

-cherophobia

i paint these chains skin color
and pretend i am free.

-imprisoned

when this heart stops beating
and my face goes cold
lay me to rest in a garden of darlings.
where love flows through the soil
and feeds the trees.
leave my stone unmarked
so visitors are forced to wonder
and dream ideas of who i was.

i hope in their stories, i found peace.
i hope in their stories, i was loved.

-help me rest

i don't know which hurts more.

the quick deaths. the dropped bombs and blast waves.
those swift fractures that leave you screaming.

or is it the slow bleedouts. a thousand bee stings.
the same spot bruised over and over. until the skin breaks.

but what hurts worse than the blindsides
or the gradual decays
is suffering both.

-ways to break

poetry is only heartache and metaphors.

-at least mine is

i don't care for big cities and tall buildings.
they make me feel so small. so insignificant.
but then again so do you.
and here i am caring.

-skyscraper

i sit here and hope the dim lighting will conceal
the bags under these hazel eyes.
they may be drained but below them is where i store
my exhaustion and self-loathing.

my hair is a mess and this mascara is from yesterday.
but there will always be predatory attention
and eyes burning holes into me.

no one knows the amount of hatred i've had for this body
as i wrap it in a skintight facade.
they did not see me an hour earlier curled up naked
in a tub made of cracked porcelain.
soaking in shame and bathing in self-deprecation.

i sip a glass of cheap wine and scribble thoughts on paper.
wishing this ink was blood as they approach me
and attempt to call this empty shell beautiful.

soon, i will slither back to my room and crawl into bed.
i look forward to the bleached sheets and nightmares.

-hotel bar

my eyes are burning
with saltwater and heat.
each drop filled with
my wandering love for you.
etching riverbeds into my cheeks.

-lava tears

on my knees
forehead kissing floor.
begging for the misery to end.

i cannot help but wonder
how many people i have collapsed
and made pray to gods
they do not believe in.

if you were sent to break me
and teach me a lesson
please tell the universe
i have learned it.

-karma

losing you.
wet concrete funneled into
the veins of my heart.
filling it with the weight of grief
and feeling it turn to stone.

-heaviness

i am piling our belongings and memories
on the living room floor.
watch me bathe in kerosene
and lie naked
on this heap of chaos.

come love.
strike a match across my collarbone
and set this mess on fire.

after the evidence of us is incinerated
and the flames have devoured all proof
i want you to eat the ashes.
handfuls at a time.

you have always tried to consume me.
so come love.
now is your chance.

-cremated

write your i love you's
on steamy mirrors.
to put them in ink
would be a lie.

-they always fade

let him go
when gravel in your lungs
replaces flutter in your stomach.

when you gasp at every breath
but question if you are worthy of air.

when you smash mirrors and smear bloody fists
to shroud your flawed reflection.

let him go
when the devil is more interested in your soul
than he is.

-it is time, my dear

i softly laid you down in the casket
and covered you with our favorite quilt.
surrounded by flowers that matched the color of your eyes.
our song and their fragrance filled the air.

i mixed our milestones with dirt and tossed handfuls on top.
all of our firsts and lasts sealing you inside the earth.
your grave was decorated with future plans, hopes, dreams.
beautiful yet plucked before full bloom.

i could have held onto the corpse of us forever.
but my darling, we've been dead for far too long.
you see, i did not bury the real you today.
only the person i once loved.

-your funeral

if i travel to a hundred new cities
maybe i will forget the life we built in this one.

if i see a million new faces
maybe i will forget yours.

-escapism

what does it feel like when you miss me?

do you feel empty?
with gaping holes and craters that you try to fill with other bodies
in the bed that we bought together.

have you realized yet that i cannot be replaced?
maybe you feel heavy.
so weighted with regret and grief that you would sink
straight to the bottom of the lake that we played in last summer.

have you accepted that i am not coming back?
i guess it does not matter if i understand your pain.
it will not alter how i mourn you.

your handprints are burned into my skin
so i will never forget you.
but those marks are surface wounds
and remembering is different than missing.

you left the chambers in my heart bleeding and vacant
but open for someone better to inhabit.
yours will remain lightless and unfit. yours will remain unoccupied.

-tenantless

i felt the final thread break.
the last one linking me to this body
and this body to you.

i was dying.
but i knew i had to in order to be born
into a body that you have not touched.
into a world where you do not
e x i s t.

-necessary death

it's funny how i thought i needed you
and ignored the way you cut me open and bled me out.

i just wanted to feel the heat of someone's body next to mine
even if it blistered my skin.
to have a mouth that kissed and breathed empty promises into me
like poison gas.

i believed you were the key to wholeness.
in reality, you depleted all of my vigor.
such a captivating and toxic illusion.
how many times i've masked "i can't be alone" with "i love you".

to think i would sacrifice and surrender this self to you
so that i would not have to be
alone
with
it.

-attachment ≠ love

bursts of romance
glowing with affection.
then the silence and darkness
until you decide to send
the next one up.
and i sit and stare at the sky
just waiting.

-firework love

to his new partner,

you confidently wear red lipstick.
he probably hasn't told you how much he hates it yet.
you smile at night thinking about all of his romantic gestures.
he must not be bored with you so far.
you look at him and know he has your heart.
he looks at you and thinks he owns much more than that.

i could warn you about him
but i would rob you of this temporary bliss.
i could carve 'beware' into his front door
but you will need to see this for yourself.

i could be wrong.
he may have changed.
when he tells you he respects you
his lips may no longer drip with deceit.
that beautiful monster may have dulled his teeth
and stopped feeding on good women.

for your sake, i hope that's true.
he could be your blessing.
but he was

- my curse

don't be fooled
by a handsome face and soft eyes.
his skin is stained with demons
and he will grip your throat
with the same hand that brushes
the hair behind your ear.

-gentle guise

i've always been the convenient distraction.
the in-between, reserving space between the 'last' and the 'next'.

i am the caretaker, the emotional laborer, the best to talk to.
i am the fun, playful, funny, wild, free girl.
you use my ears. my body. my mind. my heart. my energy.

i am the one that teaches boys life lessons
just in time for soulmates to appear.
the catalyst of your maturation, your romantic evolution.

you will be better after me.
she will reap the rewards.

-placeholder

i am conveniently placed
in the sometimes of your love.

-timely

they will always want a taste of you.
to sample your greatness and experience an ounce of your splendor.
you are distinct and they can detect it from a mile away
like blood in the water.

they will take bites out of you
knowing that they do not want your wholeness.
they are far too curious and far too scared to miss out.

they do not respect you enough to leave you alone.
instead they leave you
with gashes and teeth marks.

-sharks

wrap me in your cloak of splinters
and trick me into thinking
you are loving me.

-swaddle and swindle

they all warned me about dangerous heights and boys like you.
but when i saw your eyes, i knew i was falling.

they all heard my heart and neck break
before i even hit the ground.

-dead on impact

you only think i am pretty when
your foot is on my throat.

-power play

to those who convinced me they were different
and it was safe to expose my neck.

to those who covered themselves in sheets
and false interest.

to those who fed until their bellies were full
then slowly dissolved away.

to those who left me questioning my worth
and inspecting my soul for every dent and stain.

you may have vanished
but the irresolution you left behind
will haunt me
forever.

-dear ghosts

i hear from you.
you must be craving blood again.

i know i am not your favorite taste
but as usual, my body will suffice.
a temporary and mediocre fix.

i have always been good enough
to quench your thirst
and never good enough
to make you stay.

-vampire

like a flat stone on water
you bounce from heart to heart.
just remember, love
all rocks sink eventually.

-skipping stone

sitting together, we pretend to enjoy
the cheap beer and even cheaper interaction.
it was exactly 365 days since the first time
that i stayed in your bed.

among the shallow conversation
you told me how much you love poker.
that deceitful faces and mind games excite you.
an accidental confession glistened in your eyes.

how did i miss the chips on the table
and the cards in your hand.
i realized this was a skill game
and i was a losing player.

-i fold

when you shave away the humiliation.
if you peel back the pain.
i am left exposed and impressed
by how well you play false.

-talented man

i cannot be surprised.
i should not be allowed to break.
even those who love you most
wrapped caution tape around you
and warned me of your capability.

i was a fool to think
you would prove them wrong
and be a good one.

-heedless

i felt you
slide me into the folder
labeled *as needed.*
i slowly moved you
into the drawer
carved with *almost.*

-refiled

you decided you had no use for my soul or innards.
but instead of letting me go free
or leaving me to rest and rot
you strung me up
and gutted me.

you wanted to keep me as an accessory.
so you needed to empty me out
and scrape all flesh and substance from within.
you only ever had interest in my outer appeal.
and now you have my hide laid out for display.

so you will soak your knife and bloodstained hands
and wait for the next one to join
your collection
on the floor.

-new rug

i will slit my own throat
before i breathe your name again.

—

so many times i was on all fours
slithering back to you
after you broke me at the knees.

when i think about you now
the only thing crawling is
my skin.

-formication

my chest caves when i think about the beginning.
the touching. kissing. long and slow.
drinking each other in like the finest wine.
i am learning that beautiful things decompose the quickest.
but this pill i am trying to swallow is caught in my throat.

when i see the difference between now and then
i feel the butterflies rotting in my stomach.
i wonder when you decided i was no longer a human
and became an object at your mercy and disposal.
or if you knew from the start that you wanted me for a plaything.

i cannot help but hope you feel it one day.
that you find the one who makes you crumble
and start to notice she kisses you quicker. and touches you less.
until you realize that you are nothing but a novelty option.

i cannot help but look forward to the day
we sit together
and gather dust.

-toy box

thinking of you is
a mouthful of spoiled milk
and soap in my eyes.

i cannot flush you out fast enough.

-rinse and repeat

my parents did not create me
for your use.

my mother did not bear and feed this body
for your pleasure.

i do not possess my father's wit and my mother's laugh
for your entertainment.

i did not inherit my grandmother's hands and compassion
for serving your needs.

i was not born
for you.

-you are not my purpose

maybe i should be grateful
for everything.
for all that you have done to me.

after all
you have given me so much
to write about.
may this version of you
live forever
in my poetry.

even long after
you have swallowed
your last victim.

-never forget the monster in you

i fear the day when
i finally stand next to a good man
and think of you.

-intrusive thought

to the men that have tasted me,

when you read my poetry
do you wonder which one you are?

a.) the parasite that invades my body
and infects my blood for its own survival.
b.) the prey that i feed on
when i'm feeling empty and carnivorous.
c.) the twin flame that could resuscitate these lungs and heart
ten years after death.
d.) the insignificant that i've not bothered to waste my ink on
beyond this very sentence.

(hint: if you are unsure, rule out the top 3 options)

-multiple choice

there are probably piles of us.
the gallons of blood
that have raced through veins
after the dozens of ears
heard your cheap lines.
i bet your mouth and ego smirked
every time another one fell
onto the stack.

-mass grave

girls like me do not forget.
instead we etch tallies under our skin
for each time you disrespect/belittle/overpower/take advantage.
we are not heavenly creatures like some.
those sweet girls forgive and leave doors open for you to return.

girls like me whisper your name at night.
loud enough for your demons to hear
and quiet enough for your angels to miss.

one day, you will pray to your god that i come back.
save your breath, love.
he is not the one who created me.

-hellish

hurricane women like me crush men like you.
the ones threatened by our force
or oblivious to our power.

we shatter you like glass.
then we chew on the shards
and spit blood for fun.

just waiting for tornadoes
to come along
and match us.

-break even or break

don't worry about how many people i have been with.
this is not a ranking system
and i am not a tournament.

a number will not reveal anything about who i am.
but asking me for one will tell me a lot
about you.

-body count

i live in a world where people want to tear
the meat from my bones.
where i am told that i should melt and boil this body down
and reduce it to nothing.

the standards keep changing
and i struggle to map out where my curves are allowed.
being a woman in this world is an exhausting sport
and i do not want to play anymore.

instead, i want a person to lay their head on my belly
and not expect me to suck it in.
i want them to look up at me without disappointment
when they see extra flesh where a defined jawline could be.

i want a world where there are no conditions to loving my body.
where every centimeter of this skin is worshiped always.
not just when it fits the latest trend.

my segments and pieces will not be your flavors of the week.
because i am more than the sum of my parts.
because this whole body is the

-flavor of the century

go ahead, blame it on daddy issues
and tell us were hysterical.
say anything to exonerate yourself.

you cauterize our bleeding wounds
by branding them with iron guilt.
you add heat and wind to our calm oceans
and then condemn us for responding
like cyclones.

all too often, you will find
behind a crazed woman
is a man gaslighting
her spine.

-overreacting

do not compare me to a light breeze.
i am the hurricane with burning winds and violent force.
i am not a sweet wine.
i am the poison that your cells will fatally absorb.

do not compare me to a flower.
i am the thorns that draw your blood.
i am not a pleasant fragrance.
i am the black smoke that will burn your lungs
and coat your insides.

do not compare me to a glowing ember.
i am fire and brimstone.
i am not delicate.
i am deadly.

do not compare me to
-soft things

seeing things break
does not mean
you are broken

-witness

i love when you call me a sweet little girl.
you don't suspect a thing and your naivety pleases me.
assume i am like the rest, it only makes it easier to close in.
it is not until you view me as prey that you will strike.

but when you cut me you will not see blood or tears.
you will watch the wound release black sludge.
all color in my eyes will drain and glaze over.
a grin will appear across my face.
and this is when you will realize you've made a mistake.
the moment you recognize that this sweet little girl
will be the one to devour you whole.

you were right.
i would never harm a fly.
i have too much fun with boys
like you.

-demon

why would i be superstitious
or shy away from
bad omens.

after all
you crossed my path on a faultless evening
without a warning or sign.

i must have been born with bad luck.
so i welcome the black cats, broken mirrors, and cursed days.

-friday the 13th

two days after writing a poem
about bad luck and curses
my mother completed suicide.

-sunday the 15th

Blood Loss

and here i've been
writing about heartache.
little did i know
i had not yet truly experienced it
until i lost you.

-ignorance was bliss

when i write about romance
i speak of blood spilling and bones breaking.
eating flesh and burning souls.
torment and poison.

but not when i write about this.
there is no carnage. no gore.
because what could be more gruesome

-than me losing you

i could say it a million times
until my voice cracks and my throat burns.
i could write a thousand poems
until my hand cramps and my fingers bleed.
i could look at you for days without breath
until i cry in pain and you still don't reach for me.
i could do all of these things
and i will still not accept
that you are gone.

-this cannot be real

so many times she told me
i don't need anyone to be happy.
i believed her until today.

-she was the exception

when my grandmother slipped away
early one morning
you told me that you couldn't bear
to see my broken look
and lost eyes.

i hope you don't see my face now.
your soul needs to rest.

-look away for a while

such a different type of grief.
a bone crushing pain.

i do not anticipate the day it stops hurting.
i do not expect a moment i will not miss you.
there is no space for something better
because you were the best.

this grief is endless.
this grief is a sad future

-without you

rewind the time.
bring me back.
let me replace your life
with my hand.

-please take that instead

did you know that when i was in your belly
i passed my tiny cells to you?
and they traveled to your bones. mind. lungs. heart.
people talk about what a mother passes to her child
yet this small trade is overlooked.

so you were right when you said
that i lived inside of you.
and i am right when i say
that a part of me died with you that day.

-you took me with you

i took for granted
my access to you.
your voice, a call.
your face, a drive.
your hand, a movement.

i am left here worlds away
searching for signs of you.
questioning every flicker of light
and whisper in the breeze.
begging for a glimpse of you
still with me.

-unreachable

oh how i wish it was you rocking me to sleep
and not these waves of grief.

-rough seas

my ears have heard your heartbeat
from every angle.
and i've never heard
a sweeter song.
how quiet is this world
without it playing.

-the saddest silence

i am sorry

if i barely smile when you make a joke.
even the muscles in my face are weeping.
if i look through you while you speak.
i am seeing her face.
if i am acting differently around you.
i am tired from the nightmares.
if i talk about her every chance i get.
it is the only way to keep her alive in my heart.

i am sorry if i do these things.
i am re-learning how to be.

-i am sorry for this grief

please forgive me
for everything i did that made you feel
any less than perfect.
and for all i didn't do to show you that
you were the best.

-if guilt could kill

i know i was lucky to be yours in this life.
and i might be greedy to ask
to be your daughter again.
with your smile and laugh.
your soft soul.
your healing words.
i will hold your hand tighter
and sit with you longer.
grant me this and i promise
our next life together
will be better.

-you'll stay next time

i don't understand how nothing happened.
the earth didn't shake.
the ground didn't split.
the light didn't die.
at the moment her soul left her body
it was only our world
that ended.

-and yours goes on

take my eyes. remove my tongue.
detach each arm. both legs.
cut me in half. into quarters.
i will still feel more whole
than i did on the day you left.

than i do right now.

-completely incomplete

put your head on my shoulder
and your hand on mine
while i write poems
about you being gone.
when my heart drops too low
or stirs too fast
reach into my chest
and hold it.
please don't let go
until i stop crying.
please don't let go

-until it stops beating

memories of
me biting into lemons
and you biting tomatoes.
juice escaping from our laughing smiles.

sweet like these moments.
salty like these tears.
sour like these future days.

-the taste of missing you today

you gave me lungs
and guided my first steps.
now i'm forced to learn again
how to breathe
and navigate this world
in your absence.

-i don't know how

forever.
it is welcomed by so many.
to me
forever is a long time
to gasp for air.

-shared lungs

i am angry with the world
and the god you believe made it.
the one who let a woman drown in pain
and be crushed by suffering.
i want to burn this place to the ground
for convincing an angel that she did not belong.
tell me she is in a better place.
with a world and god this cruel
i can only beg that it's true.

-you didn't deserve her

a dream.
seeing her face and holding her hand.
a nightmare.
waking up to realize it will never be real.

-they all end up nightmares

you poured love into my heart
and from this
it produced rivers.
but your breath and love
stopped flowing
and these rivers are running dry.

-my source

please do not make me grow older
if you cannot.
i cannot bear the thought
of existing in this space longer
than you did.

-55

notes. pictures. flowers.
necklaces. rings. cards. perfume.
voicemails. poems. songs. red.

surrounded by things.

-looking for you

i want to call and tell you
how crazy life has been.
how i have hugged so many strangers
and talked to old friends.
how i saw the prettiest flowers
that you would have loved.
how i spent days with my all of my siblings
together in one room.
how i had a nightmare that you left.
how i want to share my every moment with you
like i always have.

and how i wonder if you know these things already

-because now, you're everywhere

today
i am not strong.
i am not healing.
i am not able.

today
i am a broken girl wanting her mom.

-and i will be tomorrow

you hear about the sadness.
the stinging tears and cracking hearts.
they do not warn you about the unrelenting anxiety and fear.
to wake up.
another day in this grim new reality.
to sleep.
being tricked by a dream.
you cannot truly understand
the confusion. the empty. the lost.
you carved from my future.
a hole carved into my heart.
taking so much of me with you.
i am left floating without direction.
just not high enough to see you.

-floating

i want to know who convinced you to think
you were not needed
here.

-they were wrong

"sorry for your loss"

best friend. mentor. cheerleader. secret keeper.
guardian. teacher. joker. creator. ally.
hand holder. rock. shoulder.
soulmate. mother.

"which one?"

*-losses**

you embrace the numb.
it gives you time
to blink and breathe.
but the sour stinging reality
eventually climbs out
of your heart. up your throat.
and just like that
your bubble bursts open
and the tears
spill out.

until the numb returns

-vicious circle

.

gone my love for summer days.
drinking sunshine.
devouring fresh air.
today i pray for clouds
and beg for rain.
any reason to make idleness
and dark rooms
justifiable.

-dim the world

you don't truly understand
a long-distance relationship
until the one you love
dies.

-worlds apart

you asked me to carry you
and rock you to sleep
when you were old and frail.
i promised i would.

as i hold you in my arms
30 years too early
i wonder which one of us
broke that promise.

-urn

i've feared flying
my entire life.
not anymore.
now i know what living
a real nightmare feels like.
and it isn't a crash.
now i like how close
they take me
to you.

-airplanes

the sky bright and open
yet raindrops discreetly fall.
how well the overflow is concealed
by rainbows.

-how you hid your pain

i can truthfully say
that i have loved you
since the moment we met
and continued to love you
without condition.

i only wish that you
could have seen yourself
through my eyes
and loved yourself

-like i love you

i wish this was lighter for you.
over time it may be.
but for now
it's sad and it's survival.
this is nonfiction.

-dear readers

i wonder what you're like now.
are your eyes still brown
and your smile bright.
do you still laugh.
does it make rainbows in the sky.
do you still cry when you miss us.
does it sound like thunder
and feel like rain.

are your hands still soft.
or are your wings softer.

-my angel

if we are introduced from this point forward
there is so much you may never witness.
because if you cannot meet her
then you cannot truly meet me.

she was the activating agent.
waking up my inner child.
making her giggle in bliss
and letting her cry in the safest arms.

the only light that could shine on my core
and illuminate my soul
has taken new form.
and i have too.

-dormant

while i scribble on this paper
making grief sound poetic
i imagine you tracing peaceful words
in the clouds.

i hope your poetry turns to rain
so i can feel it here on earth.

-my poet in the sky

i may visit the prettiest places.
and talk to the prettiest souls.
my mind welcomes the diversion
but nothing will ever distract this heart
from missing yours.

-engrossed

first, we shared a body.
then, we shared a life.
now, we share a soul.

-eternways

take me back
to when i only felt broken from stupid boys.
blissfully unaware of
this incurable pain.
i am used to purging the heartache.
cleansing myself of the poison
and returning better off.
this here is no cleanse.
love is bleeding from my eyes in gallons
but it does not lesson the supply.
it twists at my guts
and unhinges my heart from its cage.
to heal would mean
to be free from this anguish.
but this anguish is my love for you
and it is disastrously and beautifully
eternal.

-shattered, not broken

i hope our faces are what you saw
when you closed your eyes for the last time.
i hope peace is what you found
when you opened them in heaven.

-4 children, 2 grandkids

if you have ever loved me
then you have loved her too.

-i am her

the weight of the world made a golden heart stop beating.
but stilled gold is still gold.
and you are still you.

-stilled gold

i'm surrounded by big love.
i do know that.
but no one will ever love me like you did.
as much as you did. as hard as you did.
i do know that too.

-yours > theirs

thank you for being my first
and best love.

-you were made to be a mom

there's no way
to describe who she was
or explain how i loved her.
just as words can't replace
the sight of a sunset.
they will only fail
to capture her.

-ineffable

you left your demons here.
you can rest now.

-finally

lilacs.
a blooming so short.
but the most vibrant blossom.

-your favorite flower

grieve hard.
love harder.

-what you've taught me

i'll make sure they all know
that you were a hero. a brave survivor.
whose mind held memories
mistaken for nightmares.
you lived a lifetime longer
than most ever could.

-the war is over

i am the blend of two hurricane women.
the mother of my father.
the mother of me.
i have the salt of the earth
coursing through my veins.
my bones are made of iron and velvet.
my soul strong and soft.
full of compassion
with no room for apology.
how lucky i am to inherit
their hearts and hands.
i hope they are holding mine now
until we meet again.

-heavenly hurricanes

in the face of true loss
we recognize true love.

-parallels

there is no happy ending
but this is still a love story.

-the end

Made in the USA
Middletown, DE
14 September 2018